*Sweet Hour*

—of—

*Prayer*

© 2013 by Barbour Publishing, Inc.

Written and compiled by Donna K. Maltese.

Print ISBN 978-1-62029-730-8

eBook Editions:
Adobe Digital Edition (.epub) 978-1-62416-120-9
Kindle and MobiPocket Edition (.prc) 978-1-62416-119-3

Published by Barbour Publishing, Inc., P.O. Box 719, Uhrichsville, Ohio 44683, www.barbourbooks.com

*Our mission is to publish and distribute inspirational products offering exceptional value and biblical encouragement to the masses.*

Member of the
Evangelical Christian
Publishers Association

Printed in the United States of America.

# Sweet Hour *of* Prayer

### Inspiration from the Beloved Hymn

BARBOUR
PUBLISHING

# Contents

Introduction .......................................... 6

Sweet Hour of Prayer! ......................... 9

World of Care ...................................... 21

Wants and Wishes ............................... 33

Relief of Grief ..................................... 45

Tempter's Snare ................................... 57

Joys and Bliss ..................................... 69

Savior's Face ....................................... 83

Waiting Station .................................... 97

Winged Petition ................................. 109

Engaged in Waiting ........................... 123

Believe and Trust ............................... 135

Casting Cares .................................... 147

Consolation Shared ........................... 159

Lofty Height ...................................... 171

Seizing the Prize ............................... 183

# Sweet Hour of Prayer

Sweet hour of prayer!
Sweet hour of prayer!
That calls me from a world of care,
And bids me at my Father's throne
Make all my wants and wishes known.
In seasons of distress and grief,
My soul has often found relief
And oft escaped the tempter's snare
By thy return, sweet hour of prayer!

Sweet hour of prayer!
Sweet hour of prayer!
The joys I feel, the bliss I share,
Of those whose anxious spirits burn
With strong desires for thy return!
With such I hasten to the place
Where God my Savior shows His face,
And gladly take my station there,
And wait for thee, sweet hour of prayer!

Sweet hour of prayer!
Sweet hour of prayer!
Thy wings shall my petition bear
To Him whose truth and faithfulness
Engage the waiting soul to bless.
And since He bids me seek His face,
Believe His Word and trust His grace,
I'll cast on Him my every care,
And wait for thee, sweet hour of prayer!

Sweet hour of prayer!
Sweet hour of prayer!
May I thy consolation share,
Till, from Mount Pisgah's lofty height,
I view my home and take my flight:
This robe of flesh I'll drop and rise
To seize the everlasting prize;
And shout, while passing through the air,
Farewell, farewell, sweet hour of prayer!

WILLIAM WALFORD, 1845

Sweet Hour of Prayer!

The apostles (sent out as missionaries) came back and gathered together to Jesus, and told Him all that they had done and taught. And He said to them, (As for you) come away by yourselves to a deserted place, and rest a while–for many were (continually) coming and going.

MARK 6:30–31 AMP

10

Women are natural nurturers, always looking to fill the needs of others. Spending seemingly hour after hour *doing*—and perhaps hardly ever just *being*—we often put ourselves last on the list. Thank God for Jesus who understands that amid the world's hectic pace, we daughters of the King need time to re-center, refuel, and retool. The nurturers need to be nurtured.

At Jesus' invitation in Mark 6:31, we are called to pull ourselves away from the people and things clamoring for our attention. To turn away from the outside world and be refilled in the inner. To bring Jesus, not just our pleas and petitions, but our very presence—heart, body, mind, and soul—in prayer.

It doesn't matter what time of day it is. It doesn't matter what's on the to-do list. What matters is setting yourself down and allowing Christ to lift you up. It's time to disconnect the phone, turn off the TV, and shut the door. Take a moment—or more—each day to come away, alone with Jesus, to a deserted place, remembering that the longer a lady lingers, prayerfully present, the sweeter the sense of the Savior.

*Before daybreak the next morning,
Jesus got up and went out
to an isolated place to pray.*
MARK 1:35 NLT

*"When you pray, go into your inner room,
close your door and pray to your Father who
is in secret, and your Father who sees what
is done in secret will reward you."*
MATTHEW 6:6 NASB

*Come, my people, enter your chambers
and shut your doors behind you;
hide yourselves for a little while.*
ISAIAH 26:20 AMP

Of all duties, prayer certainly
is the sweetest and most easy.

LAURENCE STERNE

Prayer: the key of the day
and the lock of night.

THOMAS FULLER

*I will pray with the spirit, and I
will also pray with the understanding.
I will sing with the spirit, and I will
also sing with the understanding.*
1 CORINTHIANS 14:15 NKJV

*"Now My eyes will be open and
My ears attentive to the prayer
offered in this place."*
2 CHRONICLES 7:15 NASB

*The LORD is near to all who call on him,
to all who call on him in truth.*
PSALM 145:18 TNIV

## Abiding in God

Lord, I come to seek Your face,
to rest in Your presence. Fill me with
Your love and compassion. Give me
the energy to do all You have called
me to do. Quiet my mind so that
I can focus on You and only You. For
without You, Jesus, without Your love,
power, and guidance, I am lost. I desire
You like no other. And now, here,
in this place, abiding in You,
I have everything I need.

*"To you it was shown that you might know that the LORD, He is God; there is no other besides Him."*

DEUTERONOMY 4:35 NASB

*What other nation is so great as to have their gods near them the way the LORD our God is near us whenever we pray to him?*

DEUTERONOMY 4:7 TNIV

*Acknowledge that the LORD is God! He made us, and we are his. We are his people, the sheep of his pasture.*

PSALM 100:3 NLT

Of all things, guard against neglecting
God in the secret place of prayer.

WILLIAM WILBERFORCE

If we really want to achieve true prayer,
we must turn our backs upon
everything temporal, everything external,
everything that is not divine.

JOHANNES TAULER

Prayer is more than meditation.
In meditation, the source of strength is
one's self. When one prays, he goes to a
source of strength greater than his own.

MADAME DE STAEL

*The Lord is my Shepherd [to feed, guide, and shield me], I shall not lack. He makes me lie down in [fresh, tender] green pastures; He leads me beside the still and restful waters. He refreshes and restores my life (my self).*

PSALM 23:1–3 AMP

*Unfailing love shall follow me all the days of my life, and through the length of my days the house of the Lord [and His presence] shall be my dwelling place.*

PSALM 23:6 AMP

## A Soul Lifted

You are my Shepherd, Lord.
What a relief! Because You are in
control of my life, I can lay myself
down in these green pastures. I can
gaze upon the still and restful streams.
You restore me, giving me the peace
and strength to be the gentle woman
You would have me be. Thank You for
replenishing me in these moments.
To You I lift up my soul to
hold—forever and ever.

To give thanks in solitude is enough.
Thanksgiving has wings and goes
where it must go. Your prayer knows
much more about it than you do.

VICTOR HUGO

The relationship to one's fellow
man is the relationship of prayer,
the relationship to oneself is
the relationship of striving;
it is from prayer that one draws
the strength for one's striving.

FRANZ KAFKA

Every great movement of God can
be traced to a kneeling figure.

D. L. MOODY

World of Care

*He raised us up together with Him and made us sit down together (giving us joint seating with Him) in the heavenly sphere (by virtue of our being) in Christ Jesus (the Messiah, the Anointed One).*

EPHESIANS 2:6 AMP

The gravity of this world so pulls at us earthlings that at times it's hard to shrug off the problems of today and reach the heavenlies in Christ. This is especially true for those of us who are determined to fix all problems, such is our compassion for our loved ones. Yet, through the blessing of prayer, Christ calls His sisters to rise up, take His hand, and boldly approach God.

As little children, with hearts full of forgiveness and love for ourselves and others, we can shake off our worries, rise above the fray, and come before God's throne. It is there our names are written (see Luke 10:20) and our citizenship resides (see Philippians 3:20). It is the store place of treasures (see Luke 12:33) and the outlet of blessings (see John 3:27). It is where Christ now sits at the right hand of God (see Hebrews 8:1) and stands with God's people before God Himself.

God's throne is the home of our desires, where we feel the most valued and loved, and where all hope lies (see Colossians 1:5). There we receive our calling, guidance, and plan for the day, week, month, and life. An ultimate great escape from a world of care, the heavenlies are not a place to enjoy someday, but a place to spend time in every day.

*Sell what you possess and give donations to the poor; provide yourselves with purses and handbags that do not grow old, an unfailing and inexhaustible treasure in the heavens, where no thief comes near and no moth destroys.*
LUKE 12:33 AMP

*John replied, "No one can receive anything unless God gives it from heaven."*
JOHN 3:27 NLT

*Do not rejoice at this, that the spirits are subject to you, but rejoice that your names are enrolled in heaven.*
LUKE 10:20 AMP

What is heaven, but to be with God,
to dwell with him, to realize that
God is mine, and I am his?
CHARLES SPURGEON

Absent from flesh! then rise, my soul,
Where feet nor wings could never climb,
Beyond the heav'ns, where planets roll,
Measuring the cares and joys of time.
ISAAC WATTS, "ABSENT FROM FLESH!
O BLISSFUL THOUGHT!"

Earth's crammed with heaven. . . .
But only he who sees, takes off his shoes.
ELIZABETH BARRETT BROWNING

*And he said: "Truly I tell you, unless*
*you change and become like little children,*
*you will never enter the kingdom of*
*heaven. Therefore, whoever takes a humble*
*place—becoming like this child—is the*
*greatest in the kingdom of heaven."*
MATTHEW 18:3–4 TNIV

*"The kingdom of heaven is like treasure*
*hidden in a field. When a man found it,*
*he hid it again, and then in his joy went*
*and sold all he had and bought that field."*
MATTHEW 13:44 TNIV

I am overjoyed at the bliss I find in
Your presence, Jesus. Up here in
the heavens, I see things with Your
perspective. The cares of the world are
far below me, almost trivial now, and I
am at peace. There is nothing as precious
as these moments in Your realm. Here is
where my treasures are stored and from
where my blessings come. Here I long
to linger a little longer.

*"Store up for yourselves treasures in heaven,*
*where moth and rust do not destroy,*
*and where thieves do not break in and steal."*

MATTHEW 6:20 TNIV

*For we have heard of your faith in Christ*
*Jesus and your love for all of God's people,*
*which come from your confident hope of*
*what God has reserved for you in heaven.*
*You have had this expectation ever since you*
*first heard the truth of the Good News.*

COLOSSIANS 1:4–5 NLT

Meditation is the soul's perspective glass,
whereby, in her long removes, she discerneth
God, as if he were nearer at hand.

OWEN FELTHAM

Heaven is as near to our souls as this world
is to our bodies; and we are created, we are
redeemed, to have our conversation in it.

WILLIAM LAW

A soul disengaged from the world is a
heavenly one; and then are we ready for
heaven when our heart is there before us.

JOHN NEWTON

*We are citizens of heaven,*
*where the Lord Jesus Christ lives.*
PHILIPPIANS 3:20 NLT

*So then, when the Lord Jesus had spoken*
*to them, He was received up into heaven*
*and sat down at the right hand of God.*
MARK 16:19 NASB

*Blessed be the God and Father of our Lord Jesus*
*Christ, who has blessed us with every spiritual*
*blessing in the heavenly places in Christ.*
EPHESIANS 1:3 NASB

## Lightening Up

They say home is where the heart is—
and my heart is with You, Lord,
in heaven. Thank You for allowing me
to dwell there. It is so wonderful to
know exactly where I belong—
in Your precious presence, far above
worldly cares. In You, Christ Jesus, I
long to permanently reside, for You
are the Son that shines in my soul.
You are the Light in my life.

So, when I think on God's Kingdom,
I am compelled to be silent because of its
immensity, because God's Kingdom is none
other than God Himself with all His riches.

MEISTER ECKHART

Prayer is as natural an expression
of faith as breathing is of life.

JONATHAN EDWARDS

A little faith will bring your soul to heaven;
a great faith will bring heaven to your soul.

CHARLES SPURGEON

Wants and Wishes

*Keep on asking and it will be given you; keep on seeking and you will find; keep on knocking (reverently) and (the door) will be opened to you. For everyone who keeps on asking receives; and he who keeps on seeking finds; and to him who keeps on knocking, (the door) will be opened.*

MATTHEW 7:7–8 AMP

Prayer is our way of making all our wants and wishes known to God the Father—the Master Nurturer. It doesn't matter what words we use, or if we merely groan or softly sigh, because God already knows the desires of our hearts. His all-seeing presence shines its light into the very corners of your being. His all-knowingness discerns what desires are in line with His and what wishes are outside of His will. Either way, God is eager and absolutely able to answer the prayer of you, His darling daughter. But you must be patient, for His response will come in His own time.

So Jesus urges us to never become discouraged but simply keep on asking, keep on seeking, and keep on knocking. Like the persistent widow, we're told not to lose heart, not to give up. For God, a generous and loving Father, will not fail to bring what is best to His daughters. And here is where our tenacity pays off. For she who is persistent in her prayer and confident in the love and power of her Almighty Father will have her godly desires fulfilled—all to His glory. That's a power-filled promise!

*[Jesus] told them a parable to the effect that
they ought always to pray and not to turn
coward (faint, lose heart, and give up).*
LUKE 18:1 AMP

*"I will do whatever you ask in my name, so that
the Father may be glorified in the Son. You may
ask me for anything in my name, and I will do it."*
JOHN 14:13–14 TNIV

*Take delight in the LORD,
and he will give you your heart's desires.*
PSALM 37:4 NLT

Longing desire prayeth always,
though the tongue be silent. If thou
art ever longing, thou art ever praying.

AUGUSTINE

The real end of prayer is not so much
to get this or that single desire granted,
as to put human life into full and joyful
conformity with the will of God.

CHARLES BENT

*He will fulfill the desire of those who fear Him;*
*He will also hear their cry and will save them.*
PSALM 145:19 NASB

*"Those who have will be given more,*
*and they will have an abundance.*
*As for those who do not have, even what*
*they have will be taken from them."*
MATTHEW 13:12 TNIV

*"Dear woman," Jesus said to her,*
*"your faith is great. Your request is granted."*
MATTHEW 15:28 NLT

## Deepest Desires

Lord, You know my deepest desires.
You know how faithful I have been
with what You have given me in the
past. Now I come to You again,
asking to fulfill my wants, knowing
that nothing is beyond Your power.
I am seeking Your will for my life.
I am knocking on Your door, wanting
to gain entry to a new opportunity.
May my heart's desire match Your
own as I wait expectantly upon You.

*And the Spirit gives us desires that are the opposite of what the sinful nature desires. . . . Since we are living by the Spirit, let us follow the Spirit's leading in every part of our lives.*
GALATIANS 5:17, 25 NLT

*"The master said, 'Well done, my good and faithful servant. You have been faithful in handling this small amount, so now I will give you many more responsibilities. Let's celebrate together!'"*
MATTHEW 25:23 NLT

If you see any beauty in Christ,
and say, "I desire to have that,"
God will work it in you.

G.V. WIGRAM

In spiritual things, when God has raised
a desire, He always gratifies it; hence
the longing is prophetic of the blessing.
In no case is the desire of the living thing
excited to produce distress, but in order
that it may seek and find satisfaction.

CHARLES SPURGEON

*It is God Who is all the while effectually at work in you [energizing and creating in you the power and desire], both to will and to work for His good pleasure and satisfaction and delight.*

PHILIPPIANS 2:13 AMP

*For the word of God is alive and powerful. . . . It exposes our innermost thoughts and desires.*

HEBREWS 4:12 NLT

*May He grant you according to your heart's desire, and fulfill all your purpose.*

PSALM 20:4 NKJV

# Energize Me

Lord, Your Word says that You will
energize me and create in me the
power and desire to do Your will.
You have given me so much that I
want my will to match Yours. I want to
please You in all I say and do. Open
my ears, heart, mind, and spirit to Your
Word in prayer. Make Your message
clear so that I can do all that pleases You.

Prayer is not so much the means
whereby God's will is bent to
man's desires, as it is that whereby
man's will is bent to God's desires.

<small>CHARLES BENT</small>

All who call on God in true faith,
earnestly from the heart, will certainly
be heard, and will receive what they
have asked and desired.

<small>MARTIN LUTHER</small>

Relief of Grief

Then they cry out to the LORD in their trouble, and He brings them out of their distresses. He calms the storm, so that its waves are still. Then they are glad because they are quiet; so He guides them to their desired haven.

PSALM 107:28–30 NKJV

Life is full of unexpected twists and turns. Just when we think we have it all figured out and our strategies for navigating the world are in place, something unforeseen happens, sending carefully laid plans careening out of control, if not blowing them out of the water completely. Such surprises come in a variety of forms and result in a myriad of emotions. Any loss—of a job, a romance, a loved one, financial security—can cause us deep distress and grief. Thank God there is a great big Someone who can provide relief to the wounded heart, mind, body, and soul.

By running to God, focusing on Christ, and surrendering to the Spirit, we can find an infinite supply of healing and comfort. God gives the hurting strength to weather the storm. Pouring out the overwhelming pain and grief, our tears are captured in Christ's capable hands. The Comforter rushes in, a balm to the soul. When all the dust settles and a new normalcy takes over, we realize that in the midst of our loss, we can learn a lesson: no matter what happens, there will always be a refuge where our grief turns to joy, tears to laughter, heartache to healing, weakness to strength, turmoil to peace.

*Answer me when I call, O God of my
righteousness! You have relieved me in my
distress; be gracious to me and hear my prayer.*

PSALM 4:1 NASB

*Be anxious for nothing, but in everything by
prayer and supplication, with thanksgiving, let your
requests be made known to God; and the peace of
God, which surpasses all understanding, will guard
your hearts and minds through Christ Jesus.*

PHILIPPIANS 4:6–7 NKJV

How often we look upon God as our
last and feeblest resource! We go to him
because we have nowhere else to go.
And then we learn that the storms
of life have driven us, not upon the
rocks, but into the desired haven.

GEORGE MACDONALD

Those persons who know the deep peace
of God, the unfathomable peace that
passeth all understanding, are always men
and women of much prayer.

R. A. TORREY

*The LORD will command His lovingkindness
in the daytime; and His song will be with me
in the night, a prayer to the God of my life.*
PSALM 42:8 NASB

*To everything there is a season, a time
for every purpose under heaven. . . .
a time to gain, and a time to lose.*
ECCLESIASTES 3:1, 6 NKJV

*You number and record my wanderings;
put my tears into Your bottle.*
PSALM 56:8 AMP

Lord, I feel like I'm in so deep a grief that I cannot breathe. I run to You for relief. Heal my heart that's been torn in two. Hide me beneath Your wings as I ride out this storm. Fly me to a place of peace and love. I am desperate for Your comfort and the soothing balm of Your Son's presence. Give me the strength to rise again, whole and heartened.

"*I have heard your prayer,
I have seen your tears.*"
ISAIAH 38:5 NASB

*The Lord said to him, Peace be to you,
do not fear. . . . Then Gideon built an altar there
to the Lord and called it, The Lord is Peace.*
JUDGES 6:23–24 AMP

*The prayer offered in faith will restore the one
who is sick, and the Lord will raise him up.*
JAMES 5:15 NASB

That man is perfect in faith who can come
to God in the utter dearth of his feelings
and desires, without a glow or an aspiration,
with the weight of low thoughts, failures,
neglects, and wandering forgetfulness, and
say to Him, "Thou art my refuge."

GEORGE MACDONALD

Your emptiness is but the preparation for
your being filled, and your casting down is
but the making ready for your lifting up.

CHARLES SPURGEON

*In my distress I called upon the Lord;*
*I cried to my God, and He heard my voice from*
*His temple; my cry came into His ears.*

2 SAMUEL 22:7 AMP

*Then let us arise and go up to Bethel,*
*and I will make there an altar to God*
*Who answered me in the day of my distress*
*and was with me wherever I went.*

GENESIS 35:3 AMP

## Heart in Hand

I come before You, Lord, my heart in
hand. Lifting it up to You, I ask that
You hold it, for it has become too
heavy for me to bear. From it, take all
my grief and distress. Then restore it
unto me so that I may once again be
made whole. To You and You alone I
surrender myself. May I rise again,
a conduit of Your love and light.

Dear Lord, in all our loneliest pains Thou
hast the largest share and that which is
unbearable, 'tis Thine, not ours, to bear.

FREDERICK W. FABER

When you cannot stand,
He will bear you in His arms.

FRANCIS DE SALES

Faith draws the poison from every
grief, takes the sting from every loss,
and quenches the fire of every pain;
and only faith can do it.

JOSIAH GILBERT HOLLAND

Tempter's Snare

No temptation has overtaken you
except what is common to us all.
And God is faithful; he will not let
you be tempted beyond what you can
bear. But when you are tempted,
he will also provide a way out so
that you can endure it.

1 CORINTHIANS 10:13 TNIV

We face a myriad of temptations every day—the temptation to get the last word in, to share a juicy piece of gossip, to say "I told you so," to finish off that second piece of cake, to spend money on a dress, shoes, or a purse we really can't afford. Some temptations seem rather harmless. But some can sap the joy out of loved ones. And others can forever alter the world, as proven by Eve. Because she yielded to her own desires instead of God's, the first female became the catalyst for an immense Fall. So where can we turn in times of temptation? To God and His Word.

Versed and immersed in scripture, we can discern the difference between the Shepherd's voice and that of the devil. Through memorization of the Word, we, like Jesus when tempted in the desert, can use God's Word to fight off the dark one's advances. And by abiding in Christ and prayer, we can access the power to withstand anything.

Then forearmed and forewarned, we need merely keep our spiritual eyes open. For in all temptations, God provides a way of escape. Our job? To find it and, once there, breathe in the open air.

*"And do not lead us into temptation,
but deliver us from evil. [For Yours is the
kingdom and the power and the glory forever.]"*
MATTHEW 6:13 NASB

*Jabez cried to the God of Israel, saying, Oh,
that You would bless me and enlarge my border,
and that Your hand might be with me, and You
would keep me from evil so it might not hurt
me! And God granted his request.*
1 CHRONICLES 4:10 AMP

Your state is not at all to be measured
by the opposition that sin makes to you,
but by the opposition you make to it.
John Owen

Prayer is the great engine to overthrow
and rout my spiritual enemies, the great
means to procure the graces of which
I stand in hourly need.
John Newton

In danger Christ lashes us to Himself,
as the Alpine guides do when there
is perilous ice to get over.
Alexander MacLaren

*People who long to be rich fall into temptation and are trapped by many foolish and harmful desires that plunge them into ruin and destruction.*

1 TIMOTHY 6:9 NLT

*God is our Refuge and Strength [mighty and impenetrable to temptation], a very present and well-proved help in trouble.*

PSALM 46:1 AMP

*"Keep watching and praying that you may not enter into temptation; the spirit is willing, but the flesh is weak."*

MATTHEW 26:41 NASB

# Lines of Defense

I am sinking into Your Word, Lord.
Help me to cleave to Your scriptures
when my flesh is weak. May they
jump to my mind when I face an
overwhelming urge to go against
Your will. Give me the strength to do
what You would have me do. And if
I fall, forgive me, and then help me
to forgive myself. My life is in Your
hands, Lord. Help me to keep it there.

*"I do not pray that You should take them out of the world, but that You should keep them from the evil one."*
JOHN 17:15 NKJV

*[And indeed] the Lord will certainly deliver and draw me to Himself from every assault of evil. He will preserve and bring me safe unto His heavenly kingdom.*
2 TIMOTHY 4:18 AMP

*Therefore submit to God.*
*Resist the devil and he will flee from you.*
JAMES 4:7 NKJV

In the worst temptations nothing can
help us but faith that God's Son has
put on flesh, is bone, sits at the right
hand of the Father, and prays for us.
There is no mightier comfort.

MARTIN LUTHER

God shapes the world by prayer.
The more prayer there is in the world,
the better the world will be,
the mightier the forces against evil.

E. M. BOUNDS

Prayer is the spirit speaking truth to Truth.

PHILIP JAMES BAILEY

*The Lord. . .will strengthen you*
*and guard you from the evil one.*
2 THESSALONIANS 3:3 NLT

*We know [absolutely] that anyone born of God*
*does not [deliberately and knowingly] practice*
*committing sin, but the One Who was begotten*
*of God carefully watches over and protects him*
*[Christ's divine presence within him preserves*
*him against the evil], and the wicked one does*
*not lay hold (get a grip) on him or touch [him].*
1 JOHN 5:18 AMP

## A Will and a Way

When I abide in You, Jesus, no evil,
no temptation can lay a hand on me!
What an awesome fact! And when I
feel myself weakening, I know I can
come to You in prayer for strength,
courage, and determination to remain
in Your will and go Your way. Keep
my feet on Your path, my eyes on
Your face, myself in Your presence,
my hand out of the cookie jar.

It seems to me that if we get one look at Christ in His love and beauty, this world and its pleasures will look very small to us.

D. L. MOODY

God delights in our temptations, and yet hates them; he delights in them when they drive us to prayer; he hates them when they drive us to despair.

MARTIN LUTHER

Joys and Bliss

(For it is He) Who rescued and saved us from such a perilous death, and He will still rescue and save us; in and on Him we have set our hope (our joyful and confident expectation) that He will again deliver us (from danger and destruction and draw us to Himself).

2 CORINTHIANS 1:10 AMP

The media constantly feeds the message that in order to be happy, we need to look younger, sexier, and more fashionable. In other words, "You will never be good enough 'as is.'" Unfortunately, if we're focused on the world's view of all that we are not, depression and despondency are bound to set in.

But as Christians, we have a friend named Jesus, a man with a history of rescuing His people from the world and its strictures. As He was with Shadrach, Meshach, and Abednego, Christ is with His followers even in the fire, enabling us to not only escape the furnace, but to do so with neither singe nor smell of smoke. He is and will forever be the eternal, *true* lifesaver of all who believe. What joy this fact gives to us, women of the way who listen to *His* message *alone*!

Unlike happiness, which depends on circumstances, this joy in Christ is available to God's daughter who knows there's only one person to please—God Himself. As we continually, confidently, and expectantly walk with Christ, we step around the world's dangerous pitfalls and find overwhelming joy, a spring that drenches our core so we can bless others.

*Let all those who take refuge and put their trust in You rejoice; let them ever sing and shout for joy, because You make a covering over them and defend them; let those also who love Your name be joyful in You and be in high spirits.*

PSALM 5:11 AMP

*"You have made known to me the ways of life; You will make me full of gladness with Your presence."*

ACTS 2:28 NASB

## Standing in His Presence

Jesus, I am overwhelmed with joy,
knowing that as I abide in You,
nothing can move me. You keep
me safe from gossip, loss, sorrow,
backbiting, covetousness, and other
weapons of destruction. In Your
presence I long to remain, for in You
alone do I live, move, and have my
being. Teach me to pray You into me.
Joyful am I as I stand in Your presence.

"Just as the Father has loved Me, I have also loved you; abide in My love. If you keep My commandments, you will abide in My love; just as I have kept My Father's commandments and abide in His love."

JOHN 15:9–10 NASB

"The LORD your God is in your midst, a victorious warrior. He will exult over you with joy, He will be quiet in His love, He will rejoice over you with shouts of joy."

ZEPHANIAH 3:17 NASB

Prayer covers the whole of man's life.
There is no thought, feeling, yearning,
or desire, however low, trifling, or vulgar
we may deem it, which if it affects our
real interest or happiness, we may not lay
before God and be sure of sympathy.

HENRY WARD BEECHER

I would have no desire other than
to accomplish thy will. Teach me
to pray; pray thyself in me.

FRANCOIS FENELON

We have no joy but in Christ.

MATTHEW HENRY

*If they obey and serve Him, they shall
spend their days in prosperity and their
years in pleasantness and joy.*
JOB 36:11 AMP

*Without having seen Him, you love
Him; though you do not [even] now
see Him, you believe in Him and exult
and thrill with inexpressible and glorious
(triumphant, heavenly) joy.*
1 PETER 1:8 AMP

*You have endowed him with eternal blessings
and given him the joy of your presence.*
PSALM 21:6 NLT

# Total and Complete Joy

Even though I never met You
physically, Lord, I believe in You with
my entire heart, mind, body, spirit, and
soul. You make my heart sing! I have
joy in Your presence! In You I am safe.
To You I run. You are my refuge, my
strength, my stronghold, my source of
total and complete joy. You alone I long
to please. May Your name be praised!

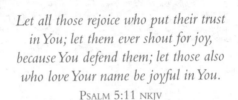

*Let all those rejoice who put their trust
in You; let them ever shout for joy,
because You defend them; let those also
who love Your name be joyful in You.*
PSALM 5:11 NKJV

*Be not grieved and depressed, for the joy
of the Lord is your strength and stronghold.*
NEHEMIAH 8:10 AMP

*I will shout for joy and sing your praises,
for you have ransomed me.*
PSALM 71:23 NLT

There is a joy which is not given
to the ungodly, but to those who love
Thee for Thine own sake, whose joy
Thou Thyself art. And this is the happy
life, to rejoice to Thee, of Thee, for Thee;
this it is, and there is no other.

AUGUSTINE

To be in Christ is the source of the
Christian's life; to be like Christ is
the sum of His excellence; to be
with Christ is the fullness of His joy.

CHARLES HODGE

Up to this time you have not asked a
[single] thing in My Name [as presenting
all that I Am]; but now ask and keep on
asking and you will receive, so that your joy
(gladness, delight) may be full and complete.

JOHN 16:24 AMP

"I have told you these things so that you will be
filled with my joy. Yes, your joy will overflow!"

JOHN 15:11 NLT

## Multitude of Blessings

To You I am pledged, Lord. Nothing
can come between us. Although
I may experience sorrow in my
circumstances, it cannot touch the
joy I have in You. Amid trouble and
mayhem, I remain still in Your calm
waters. I see Your hand in every part of
my life. You crowd me with a multitude
of blessings, with gifts I can never repay.
Amid this abundance, I revel in the joy
You continually give me.

Happiness is caused by things that happen
around me, and circumstances will mar it;
but joy flows right on through trouble; joy
flows on through the dark; joy flows in
the night as well as in the day; joy flows all
through persecution and opposition.

D. L. Moody

Seek to cultivate a buoyant,
joyous sense of the crowded
kindnesses of God in your daily life.

Alexander MacLaren

Savior's Face

*If My people, who are called by My name, shall humble themselves, pray, seek, crave, and require of necessity My face. . .then will I hear from heaven, forgive their sin, and heal their land.*

2 CHRONICLES 7:14 AMP

Sometimes we simply want to be loved. God is the same way. So He asks us to seek His face. "Seeking His face" means entering God's presence with no other agenda but to spend time with Him. In these moments, we're not asking Him to carry our burdens. We're not asking for Him to come to our rescue. And we're not asking Him to do something for us. It is merely His daughter humbling herself and coming to Him to "pray, seek, crave, and require" His face out of *her* necessity.

Oftentimes a child seeks out her mother's presence for no other reason than wanting to be with her. Her arms open wide as soon as Mommy walks into the room. Out of a need that is all encompassing, she craves her mother's face, presence, love, and warmth. And the child has no rest until she reaches her, perhaps even crying until Mommy bends down, scoops her up, and enfolds her in her arms, sharing her warmth with the child she has borne.

God would have us—His daughters—seek His face and desire His presence in the same way a child craves that of her loving mother. All we need do is pray, seek, and crave His face, and God's response will be swift and wondrous as He leans down from heaven, opens His arms, and scoops us into His all-loving presence.

*"Can a woman forget her nursing child, and not
have compassion on the son of her womb? Surely
they may forget, yet I will not forget you."*
ISAIAH 49:15 NKJV

*Seek, inquire of and for the Lord, and crave
Him and His strength (His might and
inflexibility to temptation); seek and require His
face and His presence [continually] evermore.*
PSALM 105:4 AMP

*"You cannot become my disciple without
giving up everything you own."*
LUKE 14:33 NLT

## Nothing More, Nothing Less

Lord, I come seeking Your face
today—nothing more, nothing less.
I have no petitions, no complaints,
no pleas. I merely crave Your presence,
Your strength, and Your peace. I want
to rest quietly here with You, feeling
Your arms around me and allowing
Your love to fill me up. Here, with
You, I am content to simply be. There
is nothing to do—there is merely You.

"Listen to Me. . .[you] who have been upheld by Me from birth, who have been carried from the womb: Even to your old age, I am He, and even to gray hairs I will carry you! I have made, and I will bear; even I will carry, and will deliver you."

ISAIAH 46:3–4 NKJV

Those who are led by the Spirit
of God are the children of God.

ROMANS 8:14 TNIV

Those who know God the best are
the richest and most powerful in prayer.
Little acquaintance with God,
and strangeness and coldness to Him,
make prayer a rare and feeble thing.

E. M. BOUNDS

To fall in love with God is the
greatest of all romances; to seek Him,
the greatest adventure; to find him,
the greatest human achievement.

AUGUSTINE

God is eagerly watching with
hungry eyes for the quick turn
of a human eye up to Himself.

SAMUEL GORDON

*For thus says the LORD: "Behold, I will extend peace to her like a river, and the glory of the Gentiles like a flowing stream. Then you shall feed; on her sides shall you be carried, and be dandled on her knees. As one whom his mother comforts, so I will comfort you."*
ISAIAH 66:12–13 NKJV

*"You will seek Me and find Me when you search for Me with all your heart."*
JEREMIAH 29:13 NASB

# Light and Love

I have sought You, Lord, and now I have found You. Here in this quiet space, I love and am loved. I imagine You bending down, scooping me into Your arms, and holding me close. I am melting into You and feel a sense of overwhelming peace, not knowing where You begin and I end. It is as if I am already in paradise, full of light and love.

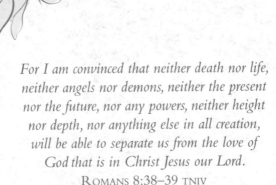

*For I am convinced that neither death nor life,
neither angels nor demons, neither the present
nor the future, nor any powers, neither height
nor depth, nor anything else in all creation,
will be able to separate us from the love of
God that is in Christ Jesus our Lord.*

ROMANS 8:38–39 TNIV

*Seek the Lord and His strength;
yearn for and seek His face and to
be in His presence continually!*

1 CHRONICLES 16:11 AMP

The spirit of prayer is a pressing forth
of the soul out of this earthly life,
it is a stretching with all its desire after
the life of God, it is a leaving, as far as it
can, all its own spirit, to receive a spirit
from above, to be one life, one love,
one spirit with Christ in God.

WILLIAM LAW

*"You neglected the Rock who had fathered you;*
*you forgot the God who had given you birth."*

DEUTERONOMY 32:18 NLT

*You have said, Seek My face [inquire for*
*and require My presence as your vital need].*
*My heart says to You, Your face (Your presence),*
*Lord, will I seek, inquire for, and require [of*
*necessity and on the authority of Your Word].*

PSALM 27:8 AMP

# Home Again

My desire for You, God, has surpassed
all others. Without You, I am lost. With
You, I am found to be loved and cared
for, as a loving mother cares for her
baby. I am losing myself in You—and
that's a good thing! Thank You for
fulfilling all my desires. In the earthly
world, I am a stranger. But here, in
Your arms, I know I am home again.
There's no place like it!

Nothing does, or can keep God out of the soul, or hinder His holy union with it, but the desire of the heart turned from Him.

WILLIAM LAW

Jesus, within You I lose myself, without You, I find myself searching to be lost again.

UNKNOWN

Nothing can separate you from God's love, absolutely nothing. God is enough for time, God is enough for eternity. God is enough!

HANNAH WHITALL SMITH

Waiting Station

*Let be and be still,
and know (recognize and
understand) that I am God.*

PSALM 46:10 AMP

Tense from stress of housework, homework, career, kids, and romance, you might become impatient to get into the presence of Christ. As you try to settle yourself, it's difficult to be still (physically and mentally) when there's so much to be done. So you reach for the Bible—the key to rising above all the noise of life—your gateway to that one-on-One focus on the Father Himself.

Soaking in the scriptures, you find your mind and soul calming, bringing your heart closer and closer to Father God's. Making the Word your own, you call on Jesus, realizing the humor in the fact that He really doesn't need to be called because He's been right next to you all along. It's just that, until then, you hadn't *recognized* Him there.

As your tension falls away, your physical eyes close and spiritual eyes open. As you seek the Savior's face, your will fades and becomes one with His. Silent and still, you experience His unconditional love and acceptance. At last, fully in His presence, you're prompted into prayer—that sweet communication, that privileged link from daughter to Father in the stillness and silence of His kingdom.

Amen.

*This Book of the Law shall not depart out of your mouth, but you shall meditate on it day and night, that you may observe and do according to all that is written in it. For then you shall make your way prosperous, and then you shall deal wisely and have good success.*

JOSHUA 1:8 AMP

*On the glorious splendor of Your majesty and on Your wondrous works I will meditate.*

PSALM 145:5 AMP

## Basking in God's Light

Father God, as I meditate on Your
Word, it soaks into my heart and works
mightily in my soul. As my spirit reaches
out for Yours, I feel Your presence, Your
peace, Your love filling me from the
top of my head to the tips of my toes.
As I bask in Your light, worldly woes
dissipate and joy prevails. Permeate me
with Your wondrous wisdom.

*So shall My word be that goes forth out of My mouth: it shall not return to Me void [without producing any effect, useless], but it shall accomplish that which I please and purpose, and it shall prosper in the thing for which I sent it.*

ISAIAH 55:11 AMP

*In the beginning [before all time] was the Word (Christ), and the Word was with God, and the Word was God Himself.*

JOHN 1:1 AMP

From faith, hope, and love, the virtues of religion referring to God, there arises a double act which bears on the spiritual communion exercised between God and us; the hearing of the Word and prayer.

WILLIAM AMES

We shall not benefit from reading the Old Testament unless we look for and meditate on the glory of Christ in its pages.

JOHN OWEN

The greatest tragedy of life is not unanswered prayer, but unoffered prayer.

F. B. MEYER

*When you are on your beds,*
*search your hearts and be silent.*
PSALM 4:4 TNIV

*Practice and cultivate and meditate upon*
*these duties; throw yourself wholly into*
*them [as your ministry], so that your*
*progress may be evident to everybody.*
1 TIMOTHY 4:15 AMP

*I will remember my song in the night; I will*
*meditate with my heart, and my spirit ponders.*
PSALM 77:6 NASB

## Pondering Spirit

Sitting in silence, I am still before Your
presence, Lord. Meditating on Your
Word, my spirit ponders. The works
of Your hands are amazing. The power
of Your Word is astounding. As I revel
in Your scripture, teach me what You
would have me learn; show me what
You would have me do; help me to
become what You envision me to be.
I desire Your will above all else.

*I will meditate on Your precepts and
have respect to Your ways [the paths
of life marked out by Your law].*
PSALM 119:15 AMP

*One thing I ask from the LORD, this only do I
seek: that I may dwell in the house of the LORD
all the days of my life, to gaze on the beauty of
the LORD and to seek him in his temple.*
PSALM 27:4 TNIV

Meditate on what you read (Psalm 119:15).
The Hebrew word for meditate means "to
be intense in the mind." Meditation without
reading is wrong and bound to err; reading
without meditation is barren and fruitless.

THOMAS WATSON

Give yourself to prayer, to reading and
meditation on divine truths: strive to
penetrate to the bottom of them and never
be content with a superficial knowledge.

DAVID BRAINERD

*For the word of God is living and powerful,*
*and sharper than any two-edged sword,*
*piercing even to the division of soul and spirit,*
*and of joints and marrow, and is a discerner*
*of the thoughts and intents of the heart.*

HEBREWS 4:12 NKJV

*I call to remembrance my song in*
*the night; I meditate within my heart,*
*and my spirit makes diligent search.*

PSALM 77:6 NKJV

Winged Petition

*Do not fret or have any anxiety about anything, but in every circumstance and in everything, by prayer and petition (definite requests), with thanksgiving, continue to make your wants known to God.*

Often we may not really know what to request of God until we have worked through the problem, pouring out our heart to the Lord in prayer. We women sometimes need to "talk it out" in order to clear our minds before we can even begin to put words to our pleas.

Consider childless Hannah who went to the temple in "deep anguish" and prayed to the Lord, "weeping bitterly" (1 Samuel 1:10 TNIV). At the end of her emptying process (prayer), she asked God for a son (petition), promising to give him back to the Lord if her request was answered. Having given over her burden and found new hope with her plea, she went on her way in peace, "her face. . .no longer downcast" (1 Samuel 1:18 TNIV). And God gave her a son.

Out of our poured-out prayers come poignant petitions. Once they are delivered, we can allow our faith to hold us up as we leave our sorrows and requests with our Friend and Father and find peace and direction. If our petition is in accordance with God's will, He will, in His time, grant our desires.

*Then Eli said [to Hannah], Go in peace,
and may the God of Israel grant your
petition which you have asked of Him.*

1 Samuel 1:17 amp

*[Hannah said,] "I am the woman who
stood here. . .praying to the Lord. For this
boy I prayed, and the Lord has given me
my petition which I asked of Him."*

1 Samuel 1:26–27 nasb

*[God] has made everything
beautiful in its time.*

Ecclesiastes 3:11 tniv

To say prayers in a decent, delicate way is not heavy work. But to pray really, to pray till hell feels the ponderous stroke, to pray till the iron gates of difficulty are opened, till the mountains of obstacles are removed, till the mists are exhaled and the clouds are lifted, and the sunshine of a cloudless day brightens—this is hard work, but it is God's work, and man's best labor.

E. M. Bounds

*"If they turn to you with their whole heart
and soul in the land of their enemies and
pray. . .toward this Temple I have built to
honor your name—then hear their prayers
and their petition from heaven where
you live, and uphold their cause."*

1 KINGS 8:48-49 NLT

*Let my prayer be set forth as
incense before You, the lifting up of
my hands as the evening sacrifice.*

PSALM 141:2 AMP

## Heart Desires

Lord, I have poured out my heart
to You—some of my prayer has
been merely groans. But with You
words are not necessary. You know
of my grief, my issues, my questions.
You know me from the inside out.
You know what I need and what my
heart desires. I want to walk in Your
will. I yearn for Your wisdom and
understanding. Help me mold my
petitions according to Your will.

*Likewise the Spirit also helps in our weaknesses. For we do not know what we should pray for as we ought, but the Spirit Himself makes intercession for us with groanings which cannot be uttered.*

ROMANS 8:26 NKJV

*The angel said to him, "Do not be afraid, Zacharias, for your petition has been heard, and your wife Elizabeth will bear you a son, and you will give him the name John."*

LUKE 1:13 NASB

Prayer is the offering up of our desires
to God in the name of Christ, for such
things as are agreeable to His will. It is
an offering of our desires. Desires are the
soul and life of prayer; words are but the
body; now as the body without the soul
is dead, so are prayers unless they
are animated with our desires.

THOMAS WATSON

Groanings which cannot be uttered are
often prayers which cannot be refused.

CHARLES SPURGEON

*With all prayer and petition pray at all
times in the Spirit, and with this in view,
be on the alert with all perseverance
and petition for all the saints.*

EPHESIANS 6:18 NASB

*"Please let our petition come before you, and pray
for us to the LORD your God. . .that the LORD
your God may tell us the way in which we
should walk and the thing that we should do."*

JEREMIAH 42:2–3 NASB

## In a Foreign Land

Lord, this world is a strange place.
I feel as if I am a foreigner in this land.
Hear my cries! Hear my plea! Search
my heart. Help me understand what
I should ask of You. I want to know
the way in which I should walk, what
I should do. Give me the strength and
wisdom that I need to fulfill Your plan
for me until I journey home to You.

*O LORD, the God of my salvation, I have cried out by day and in the night before You.*

PSALM 88:1 NASB

*In the days of His flesh [Jesus] offered up definite, special petitions [for that which He not only wanted but needed] and supplications with strong crying and tears to Him Who was [always] able to save Him [out] from death, and He was heard because of His reverence toward God.*

HEBREWS 5:7 AMP

In prayer, it is better to have a heart
without words than words without a heart.

JOHN BUNYAN

Unless the Spirit of God is
with us, we cannot expect that
our prayers will be answered.

D. L. MOODY

God shapes the world by prayer.
Prayers are deathless. They outlive
the lives of those who uttered them.

E. M. BOUNDS

*He is able also to save to the uttermost*
*(completely, perfectly, finally, and for all time and*
*eternity) those who come to God through Him,*
*since He is always living to make petition to God*
*and intercede with Him and intervene for them.*
HEBREWS 7:25 AMP

*We will sing for joy over your victory, and in the*
*name of our God we will set up our banners.*
*May the LORD fulfill all your petitions.*
PSALM 20:5 NASB

Engaged in Waiting

*Be still and rest in the Lord;*
*wait for Him and patiently*
*lean yourself upon Him.*

PSALM 37:7 AMP

124

In this I-want-it-now society, patience seems to be on a steady decline. But staying power is just what the Lord wants His daughters to have. Martin Luther said that, in Hebrew, Psalm 37:7 meant "'Be silent in God and let Him mould thee.' Keep still, and He will mould thee to the right shape."

But how do we "keep still"? By not tapping our toes in impatience. By focusing on God's will, not our own agenda. By not running ahead of God or trying to manipulate circumstances to gain what we believe we deserve.

God wants His daughters to confidently walk in faith, knowing that He will deliver *in His time*, according to His will, and always remains true to His word. If we trust in God, we have every right to expect Him to bless us, as did the lame man who "paid attention. . . expecting that he was going to get something" (Acts 3:5 AMP) and was healed! It's persistent expectation that God looks kindly upon.

Our game plan should be to continually rest in God and wait, leaning on Him at every misstep, tragedy, and heartache, knowing that no matter what happens, we may confidently expect to "see the goodness of the Lord in the land of the living" (Psalm 27:13 NKJV). Such patience and faith is amply rewarded by the God who constantly looks to find and abundantly bless His daughters.

*I waited patiently for the LORD;*
*and He inclined to me and heard my cry.*
PSALM 40:1 NASB

*I would have lost heart, unless I had believed*
*that I would see the goodness of the LORD*
*in the land of the living. Wait on the LORD;*
*be of good courage, and He shall strengthen*
*your heart; wait, I say, on the LORD!*
PSALM 27:13–14 NKJV

Never was a faithful prayer lost. Some prayers have a longer voyage than others, but then they return with their richer landing at last, so that the praying soul is a gainer by waiting for an answer.

WILLIAM GURNALL

To wait on God is to live a life of desire toward Him, delight in Him, dependence on Him, and devotedness to Him.

MATTHEW HENRY

*The eyes of all wait for You [looking, watching, and expecting] and You give them their food in due season.*

PSALM 145:15 AMP

*For the vision is yet for an appointed time and it hastens to the end [fulfillment]; it will not deceive or disappoint. Though it tarry, wait [earnestly] for it, because it will surely come; it will not be behindhand on its appointed day.*

HABAKKUK 2:3 AMP

## Attuned to the Shepherd

Lord, You know what I've been
praying for. You know every need,
desire, and longing I have. Yet I also
know that I will see Your goodness in
every situation I encounter if I just
keep my eyes on You and my ears
attuned to Your Shepherd's voice.
Thus, I have a peace that goes beyond
understanding and serenity and
patience that endures to Your glory!

*Each morning I bring my requests
to you and wait expectantly.*
PSALM 5:3 NLT

*We were given this hope when we were
saved. (If we already have something,
we don't need to hope for it. But if we look
forward to something we don't yet have,
we must wait patiently and confidently.)*
ROMANS 8:24–25 NLT

*Lord, what do I wait for and expect?
My hope and expectation are in You.*
PSALM 39:7 AMP

I think Christians fail so often to get
answers to their prayers because they
do not wait long enough on God.
They just drop down and say a few
words, and then jump up and forget it
and expect God to answer them. Such
praying always reminds me of the small
boy ringing his neighbor's doorbell, and
then running away as fast as he can go.

E. M. BOUNDS

*Roll your works upon the Lord [commit and trust them wholly to Him; He will cause your thoughts to become agreeable to His will, and] so shall your plans be established and succeed.*

PROVERBS 16:3 AMP

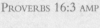

*The Lord is good to those who wait hopefully and expectantly for Him, to those who seek Him [inquire of and for Him and require Him by right of necessity and on the authority of God's word].*

LAMENTATIONS 3:25 AMP

## Never Give Up

I am confidently and expectantly
looking to You, Lord. I will never
give up hope as I wait on Your reply.
I give my life and all that I love into
Your hands, knowing that You have
only the best in mind for me. For You
are a loving Father who delights in a
faithful daughter. I thank You, Lord,
for all that You have done, are doing,
and will do in my life!

*I will listen [with expectancy] to what God the Lord will say, for He will speak peace to His people, to His saints (those who are in right standing with Him)—but let them not turn again to [self-confident] folly.*

PSALM 85:8 AMP

*For if we are faithful to the end, trusting God just as firmly as when we first believed, we will share in all that belongs to Christ.*

HEBREWS 3:14 NLT

Believe and Trust

*Let us then fearlessly and confidently and boldly draw near to the throne of grace (the throne of God's unmerited favor to us sinners), that we may receive mercy (for our failures) and find grace to help in good time for every need (appropriate help and well-timed help, coming just when we need it).*

HEBREWS 4:16 AMP

136

An amazing confidence is available to the woman who seeks God's face, believes in His Word, and trusts in the power of His grace. It gives us the same intense energy that strengthened the apostles and enabled Stephen to work great miracles among God's people.

Yet there is a paradox. For it is through our weakness that Christ's strength and power is made perfect—all enabling! Think of it! Knowing we are perfectly and abundantly empowered by God, we need not be afraid of anything as we confidently rest in Christ and live in God's love! The power of God's grace will come at the exact moment and enable us to do whatever is necessary. The seemingly impossible is now possible. This is what separates the Christians from the rest of the crowd!

Acts 20:32 says that the "Word of His grace" not only builds us up but gives us an "inheritance among all God's set-apart ones (those consecrated, purified, and transformed of soul)" (AMP). And set apart we are! We don't need to find strength and confidence outside ourselves but merely tap into Christ's transforming power from within. What an incredible lift for the woman who stands not on her own, but on God, His Word, and His grace!

*The God of all grace [Who imparts all blessing and favor], Who has called you to His [own] eternal glory in Christ Jesus, will Himself complete and make you what you ought to be, establish and ground you securely, and strengthen, and settle you.*

1 Peter 5:10 amp

*[Jesus said,]"I tell you, you can pray for anything, and if you believe that you've received it, it will be yours."*

Mark 11:24 nlt

All Christian power springs from
communion with God and from
the indwelling of divine grace.

JAMES H. AUGHEY

Remember that vision on the Mount of
Transfiguration; and let it be ours, even in
the glare of earthly joys and brightnesses, to
lift up our eyes, like those wondering three,
and see no man any more, save Jesus only.

ALEXANDER MACLAREN

Grace is given not because we have
done good works, but in order that
we may be able to do them.

AUGUSTINE

*And the Word became flesh and dwelt among us,
and we beheld His glory, the glory as of the only
begotten of the Father, full of grace and truth.*
JOHN 1:14 NKJV

*"The seed in the good soil, these are
the ones who have heard the word in
an honest and good heart, and hold it
fast, and bear fruit with perseverance."*
LUKE 8:15 NASB

# Confident and Powerful

Lord, because I believe in Your Word and trust Your grace, I can be strong even when I feel the weakest. All I need to do is look to You as You abide within. Because You are always with me, I need not be afraid in any situation. Thus, I am confident in all things. How wonderful, knowing that Your power rests upon me—now and forever!

Jesus told them, "This is the only work God wants from you: Believe in the one he has sent."

JOHN 6:29 NLT

[The Lord] said to me, "My grace is sufficient for you, for My strength is made perfect in weakness." Therefore most gladly I will rather boast in my infirmities, that the power of Christ may rest upon me.

2 CORINTHIANS 12:9 NKJV

"Don't be afraid; just believe."

MARK 5:36 TNIV

Faith has nothing to do with feelings or
with impressions, with improbabilities or
with outward experiences. If we desire
to couple such things with faith, then we
are no longer resting on the Word of God,
because faith needs nothing of the kind.
Faith rests on the naked Word of God.
When we take Him at His Word,
the heart is at peace.

GEORGE MUELLER

Grace is the free, undeserved goodness
and favor of God to mankind.

MATTHEW HENRY

*Blessed (happy, fortunate, to be envied) are
all those who [earnestly] wait for Him, who
expect and look and long for Him [for His
victory, His favor, His love, His peace, His joy,
and His matchless, unbroken companionship]!*
ISAIAH 30:18 AMP

*"Blessed is she who believed that there
would be a fulfillment of what had
been spoken to her by the Lord."*
LUKE 1:45 NASB

## At His Word

I am taking You at Your word today
and every day, Lord. I am no longer
leaning on anything outside of You.
You are a God of truth, light, and
blessings. Thank You so much for Your
Son and the grace You have bestowed
upon me. Looking not to my own
power, but solely to Yours within, I
have peace, knowing I have all the
strength I need whenever I need it
today and forever.

*It is by free grace (God's unmerited favor) that you are saved. . .through [your] faith. And this [salvation] is not of yourselves [of your own doing, it came not through your own striving], but it is the gift of God.*

EPHESIANS 2:8 AMP

*I pray that God, the source of hope, will fill you completely with joy and peace because you trust in him. Then you will overflow with confident hope through the power of the Holy Spirit.*

ROMANS 15:13 NLT

Casting Cares

The Lord said to her, "My dear Martha, you are worried and upset over all these details! There is only one thing worth being concerned about. Mary has discovered it, and it will not be taken away from her."

LUKE 10:41–42 NLT

All the "what if" supposing in life can leave a person bereft of peace. For that worrywart's focus is no longer on the Word and frame of one called Jesus Christ but is on the myriad of possibilities that may never actually happen. What a waste of God-given energy for the distracted diva whose song of trust, triumph, and tranquility is being drowned out by worldly woes.

Better that we be like Mary who sought and was concerned about only one thing—dwelling in God's Word, beholding His beauty, and meditating in His temple (see Psalm 27:4). When we're in His presence, no evil, no worry, no "what ifs" can reach us. He is a strong tower, a refuge, a depository for our cares.

Caretaker is defined as "a person who takes care of a vulnerable person, often a close relative." It is a wise woman who accepts Jesus Christ as the taker of her cares. She knows that when she commits herself—mind, body, spirit, soul, and heart—and her life to the Lord, she is in the best of places, reposing at His feet, listening to His voice, praising His name, and simply resting, trusting He will see her through every situation. Blessed is the woman who allows Christ to be her Caretaker—in this life and the next.

"Blessed are those who trust in the L<small>ORD</small>, whose confidence is in him. They will be like a tree planted by the water that sends out its roots by the stream. It does not fear when heat comes; its leaves are always green. It has no worries in a year of drought and never fails to bear fruit."

J<small>EREMIAH</small> 17:7–9 <small>TNIV</small>

My desire is to have you free from all anxiety and distressing care.

1 C<small>ORINTHIANS</small> 7:32 <small>AMP</small>

Our lives are full of supposes. Suppose this should happen, or suppose that should happen; what could we do; how could we bear it? But, if we are living in the high tower of the dwelling place of God, all these supposes will drop out of our lives. We shall be quiet from the fear of evil, for no threatenings of evil can penetrate into the high tower of God.

HANNAH WHITALL SMITH

*God has visited His people [in order to help and care for and provide for them]!*
LUKE 7:16 AMP

*[Cast] the whole of your care [all your anxieties, all your worries, all your concerns, once and for all] on Him, for He cares for you affectionately and cares about you watchfully.*
1 PETER 5:7 AMP

*So we fasted and earnestly prayed that our God would take care of us, and he heard our prayer.*
EZRA 8:23 NLT

## Continual Caretaker

How awesome to know, Lord, that from
the day of my birth You have been caring
for me. And that You will continue to do so
throughout my life. Because You will always
be here for me, I need not worry about
anything. Help me, Lord, to keep that
thought in the forefront of my mind. Help
me to realize that the concerns I have for
today are only passing, but You are forever.

*"Do not be worried about your life."*
MATTHEW 6:25 NASB

*"I will be your God throughout your lifetime—until your hair is white with age. I made you, and I will care for you. I will carry you along and save you."*
ISAIAH 46:4 NLT

*"Even when you are chased by those who seek to kill you, your life is safe in the care of the LORD your God, secure in his treasure pouch!"*
1 SAMUEL 25:29 NLT

It is of no use to say to men, "Let not
your heart be troubled," unless you
finish the verse and say, "Believe
in God, believe also in Christ."

ALEXANDER MACLAREN

Worry is a thin stream of fear that trickles
through the mind, which, if encouraged,
will cut a channel so wide that all other
thoughts will be drained out.

UNKNOWN

The sovereign cure for worry is prayer.

WILLIAM JAMES

*"You gave me life and showed me your unfailing love. My life was preserved by your care."*
JOB 10:12 NLT

*And this same God who takes care of me will supply all your needs from his glorious riches, which have been given to us in Christ Jesus.*
PHILIPPIANS 4:19 NLT

*I will be glad and rejoice in your unfailing love, for you have seen my troubles, and you care about the anguish of my soul.*
PSALM 31:7 NLT

## Standing Strong

Because of prayer, I need not panic,
Lord. I know You are watching over me.
You even send Your angels to keep me
from tripping up. And all I need to do
is call out Your name and You save me
from the wind and waves that threaten.
You, my God and Father, can help
me overcome everything—including
my fears and worries. Thus I hand
everything over to You and stand strong.

*"I am with you and will keep (watch over you with care, take notice of) you wherever you may go, and I will bring you back to this land; for I will not leave you until I have done all of which I have told you."*

GENESIS 28:15 AMP

*Give your burdens to the LORD, and he will take care of you. He will not permit the godly to slip and fall.*

PSALM 55:22 NLT

Consolation Shared

I waited patiently and expectantly for the Lord; and He inclined to me and heard my cry. He drew me up out of a horrible pit. . . . He has put a new song in my mouth, a song of praise to our God. Many shall see and fear (revere and worship) and put their trust and confident reliance in the Lord.

PSALM 40:1–3 AMP

160

When God created woman, He made her a passionate, nurturing, caring being. Because of this, we women are guilty of carrying the weight of others, especially loved ones, upon our own small shoulders. Fortunately God, keenly aware of this, provided us with a way to help lift that burden—the gift of prayer.

When we meet the Creator in prayer, the weights we carry are lifted off our shoulders. In blessed spiritual communion with the Lord, we find that faith, hope, love, and joy cannot help but increase. We're compelled to sing songs of celebration, thanking and praising God for all He has done, is doing, and will do for us and our loved ones. An overwhelming peace springs up because prayer reminds us that our current circumstances will soon be over. One day, we will be called homeward to live with our Father forever in mansions of glory. But for now, we are comforted knowing prayer is the bridge between this world and the next, and will forever be a privilege and spirit booster to everyone who wholeheartedly relies on her Creator.

*This is my comfort and consolation
in my affliction: that Your word has
revived me and given me life.*

PSALM 119:50 AMP

*All praise to God, the Father of our Lord Jesus
Christ. God is our merciful Father and the
source of all comfort. He comforts us in all our
troubles so that we can comfort others. When
they are troubled, we will be able to give them
the same comfort God has given us.*

2 CORINTHIANS 1:3–4 NLT

If we have not quiet in our minds,
outward comfort will do no more for us
than a golden slipper on a gouty foot.

JOHN BUNYAN

The beginning of anxiety is the
end of faith, and the beginning of
true faith is the end of anxiety.

GEORGE MULLER

The strong hands of God twisted the
crown of thorns into a crown of glory;
and in such hands we are safe.

CHARLES WILLIAMS

*The Lord will give [unyielding and
impenetrable] strength to His people;
the Lord will bless His people with peace.*
PSALM 29:11 AMP

*For just as we share abundantly in
the sufferings of Christ, so also our
comfort abounds through Christ.*
2 CORINTHIANS 1:5 TNIV

*Be strong, courageous, and firm; fear not
nor be in terror before them, for it is the
Lord your God Who goes with you;
He will not fail you or forsake you.*
DEUTERONOMY 31:6 AMP

## A Soothing Balm

I come to You, Lord, needing Your
comfort, Your peace, Your strength.
I feel like such a stranger in this world.
My soul longs for Your presence, Your
face, Your touch. My heart yearns for
Your words, a soothing balm to the
brokenness within. Help me to rise
above this place and fly into Your waiting
arms. Oh, what peace! Be my comforter
and shield for a few minutes more.

*Commit your way to the Lord [roll and repose each care of your load on Him]; trust (lean on, rely on, and be confident) also in Him and He will bring it to pass.*

PSALM 37:5 AMP

*The effective prayer of a righteous man can accomplish much.*

JAMES 5:16 NASB

*They do not fear bad news; they confidently trust the LORD to care for them.*

PSALM 112:7 NLT

It has been well said that no man ever sank under the burden of the day. It is when tomorrow's burden is added to the burden of today that the weight is more than a man can bear. Never load yourselves so, my friends. If you find yourselves so loaded, at least remember this: it is your own doing, not God's. He begs you to leave the future to Him, and mind the present.

GEORGE MACDONALD

Anything big enough to occupy our minds is big enough to hang a prayer on.

GEORGE MACDONALD

*[Jesus said,] "I have told you these things, so that in me you may have peace. In this world you will have trouble. But take heart! I have overcome the world."*

JOHN 16:33 TNIV

*The LORD is my strength and my shield; my heart trusts in Him, and I am helped; therefore my heart exults, and with my song I shall thank Him.*

PSALM 28:7 NASB

# Hope for Tomorrow

It's unfathomable to think, Lord, that
when I call on You, You bend Your
ear down, alert and caring, waiting to
hear what I have to say. Your attention
to me, one who at times feels so
unworthy, is humbling. Please, Lord,
ease the pain of this earthly life. Give
me hope for tomorrow, and shine Your
light on today. Give me the strength
to face the world again.

*When my anxious thoughts multiply within me,*
*Your consolations delight my soul.*

PSALM 94:19 NASB

*Now may our Lord Jesus Christ Himself*
*and God our Father, Who loved us and*
*gave us everlasting consolation and*
*encouragement and well-founded hope*
*through [His] grace (unmerited favor), comfort*
*and encourage your hearts and strengthen*
*them [make them steadfast and keep them*
*unswerving] in every good work and word.*

2 THESSALONIANS 2:16–17 AMP

Lofty Height

Looking away (from all that will distract) to Jesus, Who is the Leader and the Source of our faith (giving the first incentive for our belief) and is also its Finisher (bringing it to maturity and perfection). He, for the joy (of obtaining the prize) that was set before Him, endured the cross...and is now seated at the right hand of the throne of God.

HEBREWS 12:2 AMP

Moses brought God's children to the borders of Canaan, went atop Mount Pisgah to view the Promised Land, and then died on that lofty height (see Deuteronomy 34). Commenting on this story, Matthew Henry wrote that God's law brings His people "into the wilderness of conviction, but not into the Canaan of rest and settled peace." That "spiritual rest of conscience and the eternal rest in heaven" can only be accessed through Jesus.

The Promised Land is not an actual *place* but the *person* of Christ, the reward received when we accept Him as Lord of our lives and then abide in Him—here on earth and someday in heaven. To reach that Promised Land, we can't allow earthly things and people to distract us, but look wholeheartedly to Jesus to lead us through the wilderness. Focused on Christ, we'll have all the manna and living water we need for the journey. No longer preoccupied with or drawn away by the trappings of this world, we'll ascend to a lofty height to view our true home. There, abiding in the love and light of Christ, we'll reach the peace of the Promised Land.

*On the same day the Lord made a covenant
(promise, pledge) with Abram, saying, To your
descendants I have given this land.*
GENESIS 15:18 AMP

*You belong to Christ;
and Christ belongs to God.*
1 CORINTHIANS 3:23 NASB

*And if you belong to Christ [are in Him Who
is Abraham's Seed], then you are Abraham's
offspring and [spiritual] heirs according to promise.*
GALATIANS 3:29 AMP

Our way to heaven lies through
the wilderness of this world.
MATTHEW HENRY

We are as near to heaven as we are far from
self, and far from the love of a sinful world.
SAMUEL RUTHERFORD

So that if in this life we would enjoy
the peace of paradise, we must accustom
ourselves to a familiar, humble,
affectionate conversation with Him.
BROTHER LAWRENCE

To enter heaven, a man
must take it with him.
HENRY DRUMMOND

*When he reached the land God promised
him, he lived there by faith—for he was like
a foreigner, living in tents. . . . Abraham was
confidently looking forward to a city with eternal
foundations, a city designed and built by God.*
HEBREWS 11:9–10 NLT

*Your forefather Abraham was extremely happy
at the hope and prospect of seeing My day (My
incarnation); and he did see it and was delighted.*
JOHN 8:56 AMP

# Dwelling in Christ

Lord, I feel like such a transient being
here. But when I am abiding in You,
when I allow my soul and spirit to
be dissolved in You, I know I am
truly home. This is where I always
want to be. Thank You for dying so
that I could inherit and dwell in the
Promised Land. My eyes are on You—
and not the trappings of this material
plane. What peace, what bliss!

*Then Moses went up from the plains
of Moab to Mount Nebo, to the top of
Pisgah, which is across from Jericho.
And the LORD showed him all the land.*

DEUTERONOMY 34:1 NKJV

*"I will be with you [Joshua] as I was with Moses.
. . . Be strong and courageous, for you are the one
who will lead these people to possess all the land I
swore to their ancestors I would give them."*

JOSHUA 1:5–6 NLT

Ye do well to remember that habitual
affectionate communion with God,
asking Him for all good which is needed,
praising Him for all that is received, and
trusting Him for future supplies, prevents
anxious cares, inspires peace, calmness
and composure, and furnishes a delight
surpassing all finite comprehension.

JAMES H. AUGHEY

A soul disengaged from the world is a
heavenly one; and then are we ready for
heaven when our heart is there before us.

JOHN NEWTON

*But those who wait for the Lord [who expect, look for, and hope in Him] shall change and renew their strength and power; they shall lift their wings and mount up [close to God] as eagles [mount up to the sun]; they shall run and not be weary, they shall walk and not faint or become tired.*

ISAIAH 40:31 AMP

*The LORD in his mercy will lead them; he will lead them beside cool waters.*

ISAIAH 49:10 NLT

## A Taste of Heaven

I am struggling to disengage from
this world, Lord. There are so many
things trying to distract me. When I
get caught up in the material plane,
when I lose sight of You, I feel so
lost, helpless, and alone. But then I
run to You and receive the courage
and strength I need. I delight in Your
presence and Your peace. It's a taste of
heaven, savory to my soul and spirit.

*Now those who are made of the dust are like him
who was first made of the dust (earthly-minded);
and as is [the Man] from heaven, so also [are
those] who are of heaven (heavenly-minded).*

1 CORINTHIANS 15:48 AMP

*They were looking for a better place,
a heavenly homeland. That is why God
is not ashamed to be called their God,
for he has prepared a city for them.*

HEBREWS 11:16 NLT

Seizing the Prize

*And after my skin, even this body,
has been destroyed, then from my flesh
or without it I shall see God, Whom
I, even I, shall see for myself and on
my side! And my eyes shall behold
Him, and not as a stranger!*

JOB 19:26–27 AMP

While on this side of heaven, we can reach the Promised Land by prayer in communion with Christ. But someday prayer will fall away as God calls us, His daughters, home.

Once in His mansion, our earthly bodies will be perfected, and we'll reach the haven where Christ, God, angels, and all the saints who have gone before reside! In eternal life we will see and talk with God and His Son face-to-face. In this ethereal place, filled with love and light, all will be made known.

For once, there will be no niggling thoughts about our imperfections. Impatience will fade away. Sorrow will disappear, problems dissipate. There will be no barrier between us and our heavenly Father and His Son.

And then one final day, when Christ unites the entire world with God, we will see the new heaven and the new earth, a place free from everything evil. There we will bask in the light the Lord God shines on His city.

But until those days, we may praise God that our passage to the Promised Land remains clear through the avenue of the sweet hour of prayer.

The Spirit of God, who raised Jesus
from the dead, lives in you. And just
as God raised Christ Jesus from the dead,
he will give life to your mortal bodies
by this same Spirit living within you.

ROMANS 8:11 NLT

"I speak to him face to face,
clearly, and not in riddles!"

NUMBERS 12:8 NLT

The smoke of the incense, with the
prayers of the saints, went up before
God out of the angel's hand.

REVELATION 8:4 NASB

## Happy Day

Lord, I know that someday I will be up
in heaven with You—and what a happy
day that will be, when I can talk to and
see You face-to-face. For now, God, my
Father and King, I pray for all those
who do not yet know You, especially
those that are dear to my heart. I leave
them in Your hands, comforted by the
fact that You want all to be saved.

*We are [even here and] now God's children;*
*it is not yet disclosed (made clear) what we*
*shall be [hereafter], but we know that when He*
*comes and is manifested, we shall [as God's*
*children] resemble and be like Him, for we*
*shall see Him just as He [really] is.*
1 JOHN 3:2 AMP

*But we are looking forward to the new*
*heavens and new earth he has promised,*
*a world filled with God's righteousness.*
2 PETER 3:13 NLT

Blessed is the pilgrim who seeketh
not an abiding place unto himself in
this world; but longeth to be dissolved,
and be with Christ in heaven.

THOMAS À KEMPIS

Strange that I am not ever looking up,
if I expect to see the door of heaven open,
and the One I love coming out. Oh!
what a scene, when He comes forth to
change these vile bodies, fashioning them
like to His own glorious body!

G.V. WIGRAM

*When this perishable will have put on the imperishable, and this mortal will have put on immortality, then will come about the saying that is written, "Death is swallowed up in victory."*

1 CORINTHIANS 15:54 NASB

*I heard a loud shout from the throne, saying, "Look, God's home is now among his people! He will live with them, and they will be his people. God himself will be with them."*

REVELATION 21:3 NLT

*River of Life*

I am here before You, Lord, longing
to be dissolved in You. I long for the
day when there will be no more pain
or sorrow. When You will be upon the
throne, reigning over a new heaven
and earth. You have given me eternal
life, Lord. Help me to make my years
here count until I meet You down
by the River of Life.

*Now to Him Who, by (in consequence of) the [action of His] power that is at work within us, is able to [carry out His purpose and] do superabundantly, far over and above all that we [dare] ask or think [infinitely beyond our highest prayers, desires, thoughts, hopes, or dreams]. . .*

EPHESIANS 3:20 AMP